Dog Tricks
& TRAINING

Heather Hammonds

Published by Hinkler Books Pty Ltd
45–55 Fairchild Street
Heatherton Victoria 3202 Australia
www.hinkler.com.au

hinkler

Author: Heather Hammonds
Project editor: Kate Cuthbert
Cover Design: Hinkler Design Studio
Internal Design: Graphic Print Group
Prepress: Graphic Print Group

Images © istockphoto.com: Yorkshire, Border Collie © Eric Isselée;
Images © Shutterstock.com: Border Collie hoop © Margo Harrison;
Border Collie agility course © Ventura; dog food © Marie C. Fields.

ISBN: 978 1 7418 4168 8

Printed and bound in China

This publication is an activity book designed to entertain and educate.
All activities undertaken with dogs shall be the owner's responsibility
and at the owner's discretion. Children should always be supervised
around dogs. The Publisher, the Author, the Editor, or their respective
employees or agents shall not accept responsibility for injury or damage
occasioned to any person as a result from participation (voluntary or
involuntary) in any activity in this book, whether or not such injury, loss,
or damage is in any way due to any negligent act or omission, breach
of duty or default on the part of the Publisher, the Author, the Editor, or
their respective employees or agents.

CONTENTS

INTRODUCTION

Dogs truly are our best friends. They provide us with hours of companionship, love and fun, and ask for very little in return. Our dogs enjoy nothing better than spending time with the family at work and play, or just hanging out with us.

Teaching your dog to walk nicely on a lead and be obedient is an important part of dog ownership. However, dogs are capable of learning so much more. Dog tricks are a great way for you and your best friend to have fun together and form a close bond. Dogs love to be the centre of attention and are real show-offs! Performing tricks for family and friends is very rewarding for both the dog and the owner.

This book will show you how to teach your best friend a number of different tricks in a fun, easy and positive way. It doesn't matter whether you have a pup or an older dog, any dog can learn new tricks. We begin with some basic obedience positions and simple tricks before following through with some more complex show-stoppers.

Most dogs need mental as well as physical exercise to keep them happy and healthy. Adding a few tricks to your pet's daily exercise routine can also help prevent boredom and create a more obedient dog that is less likely to be destructive when the family is out at work or school.

No matter what sort of dog you have, you and your best friend are sure to find a few favourites in the following pages. Your pet will really look forward to a small amount of time spent training before morning or evening walks and it's addictive ... once you teach one trick, you'll want to teach another ... and another!

HOW TO BEGIN

Tricks and Treats

Dog tricks are taught using a style of training called 'motivational training'. This means the dog receives a reward for the correct behaviour. For the dog, the motivation to perform the action is the reward.

To teach your dog any new behaviour, you need to make it fun for him and give him a reason to want to do it. Generally, a pat and a few kind words are not enough (though they are an essential part of training too). Whether it is shaking hands or coming when you call, a special treat at the end of the behaviour makes it all worthwhile for your pet.

When training your dog to do tricks, food rewards are best. Choose foods that your dog sees as 'high value'. This means foods that he really loves and he doesn't get at meal times. Soft foods are best as they can be swallowed quickly. The dog does not have to stop too long to chew them and thus lose concentration during training.

You may choose to use foods such as cheese, sausage, skinless frankfurts, tinned sandwich meat, devon or cooked liver. You can also buy dog treats, but ensure they are soft enough to be swallowed quickly. Treats should be cut up quite small as dogs see lots of small rewards as more important than one big reward.

It's a good idea to vary the rewards you use so the dog never gets bored with the same food. So try to find several appropriate food rewards that your dog likes and swap them every couple of days.

Marking the Moment

Treats need to be given at exactly the right moment so that your dog understands just what he has done to earn his reward. To do this, we 'pair' the treats with a special word or sound called a 'marker'. The marker marks the exact moment when the behaviour is done correctly and provides a second for you to give the dog the food reward. It is a form of communication with your dog!

A marker can be any sound, as long as it is always the same. You can use the word 'Yes' or another short, single word, followed by a treat. Alternatively, many people use a mechanical clicker as it always makes exactly the same sound.

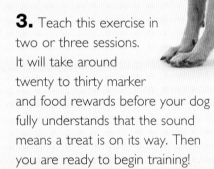

To teach your dog that the marker sound means a treat is coming, you first must 'charge' the marker. This means teaching the dog that the sound means the treat is coming. Here's how:

1. Do not ask your dog to do anything. Simply say 'yes' or click the clicker, and give a treat immediately. The treat must be given within a second of the marker for the dog to make the link.

2. Now you have Fido's attention! Repeat the marker and reward but don't try to train anything at this time. You are teaching your dog only that the marker sound means a treat is coming.

3. Teach this exercise in two or three sessions. It will take around twenty to thirty marker and food rewards before your dog fully understands that the sound means a treat is on its way. Then you are ready to begin training!

4. In the early stages of training, refresh your dog's memory by 'recharging' the marker a few times before you begin practice.

Tip

Many trainers keep treats in a bum bag for easy access to them. Try keeping some in a bum bag and some in your pocket too.

Praise and Practice Make Perfect

The secret to successfully training your dog to do tricks or anything else is to ensure that he feels very happy and confident while learning. Training time should be an extremely pleasant time for you and your best friend with lots of laughter, praise and excitement.

Here are some tips to help you and your dog learn quickly and successfully.

Keep your training sessions short. It is best to do several short training sessions than one long training session of, say, an hour, when training tricks. As a good guide, you should always finish while your dog is still motivated and wants to keep training. For beginner dogs, training sessions of five minutes are sufficient. For puppies, even less. As dogs become more experienced you can extend your training sessions but never continue until the dog is bored or no longer wants to work.

Set a clear training plan in your mind before you start. Decide which trick you are going to teach and how far you hope to progress with each training session. Stick to the plan and you will have less chance of confusing your dog and more chance of success! Remember, Fido may not achieve everything you want him to at each training session or he may achieve more. That's okay – just leave it until the next session and adjust your plan to suit.

In the beginning, train only one trick at a time. When a dog is more experienced, never train more than two tricks at a time until the dog has mastered those tricks. Then polish the tricks the dog has mastered now and again at individual sessions to keep them working well, and go on to train new ones at other sessions.

Begin to train new tricks in an area of low distraction where your dog is very comfortable, such as the living room or in the back garden. Once Fido has mastered the trick you can then begin to take it outside, to the park or other places where there are distractions like other dogs and people. At this time, Fido will have to concentrate more to do his tricks, so he needs to know them well first.

When your dog gets something right in training, as well as using the marker and reward, be very generous with your praise and pats. Make your dog feel proud of what he has just done! If Fido makes a mistake or does not quite understand something when you are training don't reprimand him or frown, or show any sign of displeasure at all. Simply withhold the marker and food reward. Reposition your dog and try again. Your dog will work hard to figure out what it is that you want him to do in order to get the reward. If you reprimand him for a mistake he will lose confidence and become confused.

Dog tricks are generally behaviours that are made up of several steps. If your dog seems to misunderstand something you are teaching him and he just isn't 'getting it' then take a step backwards and start again. You will often find he doesn't understand very well something basic and needs to revisit it in order to learn more. Also, remember that if Fido just mastered something new on one day, he may not fully remember it the next and it will take a few days of getting a trick right for it to be solid in his mind.

I always like to end on a 'high note' when teaching my dog something new. For example, if your dog is learning to shake hands and you have several tries at it and finally get two good shakes in a row, quit while you are ahead! Let the dog finish happily, with a good achievement. Don't be tempted to keep persevering on to the next step out of enthusiasm. Let Fido be proud of getting something right and wait until the next training session to consolidate it. This will help build his confidence further and motivate him to carry on learning.

PART ONE
BASIC TRAINING AND TRICKS

Before you can begin to teach your dog tricks he needs to know how to do some basic obedience positions. Here's how to train them.

Sit

Step 1
Have your dog standing up close in front of you, and have a piece of food in your hand.

Step 2
Let Fido see the food in your hand and reach for it. Slowly move the food backwards over his head and say the word 'sit'. Your dog will lift his head up and sit.

Step 3
At this point quickly mark and reward the sit, as soon as the dog's bottom is right on the ground.

Step 4
Gradually extend the time that your dog is sitting before you mark and reward. Then work on removing the food from your hand and having the dog sit, just on your command. Then mark and reward with a treat from your pocket.

Drop

Step 1
Have the dog standing in front of you and have your food at the ready, as for the sit.

Step 2
Let Fido see the food in your hand and then gradually move it forward and down between his front paws, as you say 'drop'. Your dog will put his head down and then drop, to get the food.

Step 3
Mark and reward the action once Fido has dropped right down on the ground.

Step 4
Extend the time Fido has dropped and put the food in your pocket, as for the sit.

Stay

Stay is one of the most important exercises you can teach your dog. Once you have taught Fido to stay in the sit position, you can teach him to do it when in a drop, a stand or in any other position you have him in while doing tricks.

Step 1

Have your dog sit at your left side.

Step 2

Use your left hand like a stop signal in front of your dog, palm facing him, and say 'stay' in a calm, firm voice.

Step 3

Now take one step around to face your dog, with hands folded together in front of you. Stand right in front of Fido at this point and count five seconds in your head. If he looks like moving, repeat the stay command and hand signal.

Step 4

Return to the side of your dog, then mark the end of the behaviour and reward him.

Step 5

Slowly extend the time that Fido sits in a stay in front of you, until he will sit quietly for a minute.

Step 6

Now practise slowly moving away from Fido, just a few steps at a time, until he can stay while you are some distance from him.

Tip

Some trainers also teach their dogs a second stay-type command, such as 'wait' or 'freeze'. This command is used to get the dog to hold position in the middle of a trick, for example, when they are holding something or posing for a photo.

Come

The recall exercise is another extremely important exercise that you need to teach your dog. It is used when training tricks but is also very useful at the park or anywhere you want your dog to come quickly to you.

Ideally, the recall should be one of the very first exercises you teach a new puppy. If you train the recall with a marker and food reward, puppies soon learn that every single time they run to you when you call, they get a reward. In a short time, the recall almost becomes a reflex action for them and they will turn the instant you call. Older dogs can learn this just as well too, with praise, practice and a little patience! Over time, you can reduce the need for a continuous marker and reward. Your dog will have learned it is a rewarding thing to come to you, and a pat and some praise will be enough as long as you continue to mark and reward every now and then.

Step 1
As with any new exercise, start teaching the recall in an area of low distraction, like your backyard.

Step 2
Wait until your dog is sniffing around and his attention is not on you. Then call out his name to attract his attention and hold out both arms and call, come! If necessary, encourage Fido to come by repeating his name and the command.

Step 3
When your dog runs to you, run backwards a little yourself and encourage him to end up right in front of you, with his attention fully on you. In the beginning, lure him with a piece of food if necessary.

Step 4
As soon as your dog is fully focused on you, mark and reward.

Step 7
Now take this exercise into an area of higher distraction, like the park. Try to choose a park where it is very safe for your dog and he cannot run away. Some off-leash parks are fenced and these are ideal. Unless you are absolutely sure it is a safe place and your dog cannot run away or go near a road, it is best to put a long line or long leash on him. Take care not to let it tangle around your hands or Fido himself.

Step 5
Encourage your dog to move away from you again, and repeat the exercise. Repeat it several times, from different parts of the garden. Make the recall fun. Always call 'come' in a cheerful voice with a smile on your face. Make a big fuss of Fido when he returns to you.

Step 6
If your dog does not come to you immediately, take care not to get impatient or annoyed with him when he finally does. If you show displeasure when the dog comes, he won't want to return to you at all next time. If you are having a problem, put a leash on him or move in closer to him before calling, or practise the recall just before your dog's dinner, when he is hungry and keen to get food rewards.

Step 8
Whenever you move to a new area with the recall, start by calling your dog to you from close by. Don't let him wander too far away before you ask him to come to you.

Step 9
If you are using a long leash on your dog, remove it only when you are absolutely confident he knows the exercise and will not run away.

Tip
You can also train your dog to sit in front of you when he comes in on the recall.

Shake Hands

Shake hands is a popular first trick and one that is particularly fun for children. It is possible to teach your dog to offer their left and right paw to each of your hands. This trick then becomes the basis for several more complex tricks, as you have taught the dog to 'target' your hand and can transfer this to other objects.

Step 1
Have your dog sit in front of you, then squat down facing him.

Step 2
Hold a treat in your right hand and very gently touch or tickle the top of your dog's right paw with your left hand. Do not say anything at this stage.

Step 3
The moment your dog moves his paw (even a tiny bit), use your marker word or the clicker to mark the movement and give the treat. At this stage, do not say the words 'shake hands', just mark and reward the action.

Step 4
Repeat Step 3 several times, encouraging the dog to lift his paw more and more. This may take a few sessions. Once the dog understands to lift his paw properly and offer it to you, add the words 'shake hands'.

Step 7

Next, teach your dog to offer the other paw to the other hand in exactly the same manner. The dog will now target each of your hands with his paw whenever you offer him the palm of your hand!

Step 5

Now turn your hand so that it is palm upwards and ask the dog to shake hands again, this time encouraging the dog to place his paw right onto the palm of your hand.

Step 6

Gradually work at the trick in small steps, until the dog automatically places his paw into the palm of your hand. Then gently close your hand around the paw as you shake it.

Tips

You can also try putting the food in your left hand and holding it near the dog's paw, waiting to mark the moment when the dog paws at your hand to try to get the food, rather than sniffing at it. However, you must be very accurate with your marking to catch this behaviour.

If your dog doesn't mind physically having his paws touched, you can also gently lift his paw and shake it yourself, saying 'shake hands'.

Roll Over

Roll over is another exciting first trick that is a real crowd-pleaser! Work on teaching your dog to roll over in one direction first. Then you can teach him to roll over both ways, and also roll over and over and over…

Step 1

Have your dog drop in front of you and then squat down facing him.

Step 2

Hold a treat in your right hand, right in front of your dog's nose, and very gently lure him over onto his side.

Step 3

Mark and reward this position the instant Fido does it, but at this stage do not say 'roll over'. Do this two or three times.

Step 4

Once again hold a treat in your hand when your dog is in the drop position and very gently lure him over onto his side. This time, keep luring him around so that he actually does roll over. You can also help him by rolling his legs over a little, but only do this if he is comfortable with it.

Step 5

Once your dog rolls completely over, mark and reward. Now you can add the words, 'roll over'.

Step 6

If your dog is confidently rolling over one way when you give the command 'roll over!', you can now start to teach him to roll over the other way. Repeat the process from Step 1. However, you will probably find that the dog picks this up very quickly and skips some of the steps, as he already has an idea of what to do.

Step 7

When your dog can confidently roll both ways independently, try asking for two rolls – one to the left and one to the right. Begin by asking for a roll one way and do not mark and reward, but immediately ask for a roll the other way – then mark and reward after the second roll is complete. This is called 'chaining behaviours'. You are chaining two roll-overs together.

Step 8

You can also teach your dog to do multiple rolls in one direction. First, begin with two rolls in the same direction, then mark and reward.

Step 9

Next, do three rolls in a row, then mark and reward. Add more rolls as you wish.

Tips

Some dogs are very flexible and find it easy to roll over. Others may only be able to roll one way, or are slower to roll. Be patient when teaching this exercise and remember some older dogs may have arthritic hips or backs, so be gentle.

Always make sure your pet is in good physical health before trying tricks such as this.

Bow

Most of us have seen our dogs playfully bow when waiting for us to throw a ball or start a game, or when they are playing with other dogs. Sometimes a dog will even bow when he stretches, so teaching your dog to bow formally is not hard. It is a cute trick that looks really impressive. When Fido becomes proficient at bowing, you can even bow to each other!

Step 1
Have your dog stand at your side and keep a treat in your right hand, ready to lure Fido downwards.

Step 2
Say nothing, but slowly lure your dog's nose down and slightly backwards at an angle with the treat between his paws. It is very important to do this slowly, as we do not want the dog to drop. We are asking for a bow.

Step 3
As your dog begins to move his head down and stretch his body slightly backwards, mark the movement and reward. This is very similar to the drop movement so at this stage it is a good idea to introduce a hand signal, to show Fido it is not a drop you are asking for. I use a circular movement and keep my palm face upwards, much as the aristocracy used to do when bowing to each other before a dance in the old days!

Step 4
Do Step 3 several times, each time luring the dog further and further down until he is in the bow position. If the dog cannot do this without dropping, you can gently place your left hand under his hind legs to hold him up. If he does not understand that you want him to bow, you can gently place your left hand on his shoulders and apply a small amount of pressure as you lure him down, to show him what you want.

Step 5
Once the dog has reached the full bow position, mark it and reward him immediately. At this time, once he fully understands the trick, you can add the word 'bow' and stop luring him down into position. Just use your hand signal to guide him, as shown.

Step 6

Now you can build the time your dog holds the full bow position. Ask your dog to bow and use the hand signal at the same time. When he bows, ask him to wait (or whatever word you have chosen to ask him to hold the position) for a second, and then mark the behaviour and reward him. Gradually extend the time out longer and longer, until he holds the bow position for the desired length of time.

Step 7

Finally, you can now change your position, gradually moving from the dog's side to standing in front of him if you wish. Then you can bow to each other, using the hand signal you have chosen.

Tip

To help teach your dog to bow, you can also 'capture' the bow position when out playing with him. Take a ball and have him jump around in front of you, just before you throw it. If Fido drops to the bow position while waiting for you to throw it, use your marker word and throw the ball as a reward. Fido will soon learn to bow so that you throw the ball. Once he does this, then add the word 'bow'.

Speak

Teaching your dog to speak, or bark on command, is a fun trick that dogs really love to perform. From teaching your dog the basic bark on command you can then follow on with other speaking tricks, including 'capturing' and rewarding any funny sounds the dog makes and giving them other names, such as 'say hello', as well as teaching him to count, featured on page 44.

Some dogs quite naturally bark a great deal when they are excited while others bark very little. Be persistent. Even if your dog does not bark much he will soon be speaking 'on command'.

Step 1
Have some rewards at the ready and your marker word or clicker. Do not reward your dog if he is barking at people passing your house, or at some other time when you do not wish him to bark. Only reward when he is barking when you want him to.

Step 2
Now get your dog excited! Jump up and down, run around the garden, get out his favourite toys and play with him. At this time, he may bark with excitement. If he begins to bark, hold your hand up and open and close it as shown, and say 'speak'. Make sure to be ready for this moment. (This is one of the few exercises I like to name for the dog right from the beginning, as well as including a hand signal.)

Step 3
The moment your dog barks, use the marker word or sound and reward him. Now make the signal and say 'speak' again, and work to get him to repeat the bark. Then once again mark and reward the trick.

Step 4

If you have a dog that is reluctant to bark or rarely barks at all, try making barking sounds at him yourself, as well as playing. This method, combined with excited play, has a good success rate with dogs that are shy about barking.

Step 5

Once you have your dog speaking on command, it is time to refine the trick. This is called 'shaping the behaviour' in dog-training terms. Most dogs bark several times in a row, rather than just once. Now you can teach Fido to speak only once when you ask him to.

Step 6

When you ask your dog to speak and give him the signal, quickly mark and reward after the first bark only. Do not reward multiple barks in quick succession. Just ignore the behaviour and try again if you cannot mark and reward a single bark in time. Timing of the marker and reward is critical in all training, but it is particularly important that you get it right here. Fido will soon learn that a single bark is what is required to get his marker word or sound, and treat.

Tip

Teaching a dog to speak on command will not turn him into a nuisance barker, even if he never barked much before you taught him the trick. If you reward the dog only when you want him to bark, he will quickly learn he gets nothing for barking at inappropriate times.

Hold and Carry

Teaching your dog to hold and carry items in his mouth is a fantastic trick and has multiple uses. The list of things you can teach him to hold and carry is endless – from baskets and bags to newspapers and your slippers!

Step 1
Begin by teaching your dog to hold and carry items with something soft that is more pleasant than a hard item. A soft rubber bone or dumbbell is ideal. Allow him to play a little with the toy first, at the start of training, so he is keen to interact with it.

Step 2
With the toy in one hand, sit your dog in front of you.

Step 3
Now hold the toy out in front of your dog's mouth. Do not push it into his face or he may back away. Just hold it in front of him. If he reaches forward to it, mark and reward. Repeat this step a few times, so Fido knows that reaching forward to the toy is what is required.

Step 4
Your dog may try to take the toy himself. If he does this, encourage it by marking and rewarding, together, of course, with lots of praise.

Step 5
If your dog is more reluctant to take the toy in his mouth when you present it to him, try being less formal. Wave it around a little and make a game of it again. The moment he picks the toy up, mark and reward.

Step 6

Once your dog is holding the toy in his mouth steadily for a few moments, add the word 'hold' and work on extending the time he holds it. Say 'hold' a couple of times and reward for gradually increasing periods of holding the object.

Step 7

When Fido can hold the toy in his mouth well for a good period of time, teach him to give it to you by gently taking both ends of the toy and saying 'give'. Do not pull the toy or he may enjoy a game of tug with you instead of giving it to you.

As soon as he lets go of the toy, mark and reward. If Fido loves his toy too much and doesn't want to give it up, show him the food reward. It should be high value enough that he releases the toy. Then mark and reward. In his mind you have just swapped one good thing for another!

Step 8

At this point you can teach your dog to carry the item as he is walking. You may find he drops it regularly at first, but persevere. Once Fido is holding the object in his mouth and you have said 'hold', walk backwards a little, encouraging him along with you. Say the word 'carry'. If he takes one or two steps before dropping the toy, mark and reward.

Step 9

Build on this exercise until you can offer an object to your dog and he will hold it in his mouth as instructed, and carry it about for you when you give him the command 'carry'. Then ask him to 'give' and take it from him.

> ### Tip
>
> *Dogs will often hold familiar things in their mouth but when you offer them a new one made of different material, they often spit it out. This is particularly so for hard items like plastic or metal. If you want your dog to carry something new, just begin at the beginning as if you are teaching him the exercise all over and he will quickly pick it up.*

Go Fetch

Teaching your dog to fetch is a natural progression from holding and carrying items. The key to success with this trick is to make it as fun and high action as possible in the beginning, so the dog enjoys running out to retrieve things.

Step 3
If your dog does not chase the ball, try again and run with him. When you reach the ball, make a game of it to see who can grab it first. If Fido grabs the ball, give lots of praise. Do not mark and reward, however, or he will think the exercise is finished. Gradually reduce the distance you run so that Fido is the one who gets there first and grabs the ball.

Step 4
Once your dog is happily running out to the ball and picking it up, call him back using the 'come' exercise. Some dogs will come straight back with the ball while others will drop it and return to you. If Fido drops the ball and returns to you, you still must praise him and mark and reward. He has just done the 'come' exercise correctly and this is most important! If Fido drops the ball when he returns, follow him as he goes to retrieve it, to make the distance between you shorter. Encourage him to hold the ball and carry it by using the 'hold' and 'carry' commands you taught him in the last exercise.

Step 1
Begin this exercise with a ball (or another toy that your dog is very familiar with). Avoid using sticks, as they can be sharp at the ends or splinter and cause injury to the dog.

Step 2
Show your dog the ball and wave it around a little to get him excited. Then clearly say 'fetch' as you throw it. Do not throw it too far the first time. Fido will most likely race out after the ball.

Step 7

At this stage, you can begin to ask your dog to fetch items for you that you have not thrown. Do this in an area of very low distraction first, such as the back garden.

Step 8

Place an item on the ground and let your dog see you do this. It is best to start again with a favourite item, such as a ball.

Step 9

Move several metres away with your dog and have him sit at your side.

Step 10

Now tell your dog to 'fetch' and point to the ball as you do so. If Fido does not run out immediately and fetch the ball, move closer and work to gain distance over several training sessions.

Step 5

When your dog is successfully running out, picking up the ball and returning to you, you can mark and reward. As he comes to you, hold out one hand and say 'give'. If Fido is reluctant to give you the ball, show him the treat. The instant he gives you the ball, mark and reward. At this stage, only use the words 'fetch' and 'give' when you do this exercise, rather than also including 'come', 'hold' and 'carry'.

Step 6

Now you have taught your dog to fetch with a ball or toy, try other items such as a rolled-up newspaper. Familiarise Fido with the item by teaching him to hold and carry it. Then throw it for him and ask him to retrieve it.

Tip

Some dogs love this exercise so much that a second throw of the item is a bigger reward than a piece of food!

PART TWO
GETTING SMARTER

As your dog progresses, you will be able to expand on some of the simpler tricks you taught him earlier. You will use behaviours you have already taught in some of the following tricks, which are a little more difficult.

Over time, Fido also 'learns to learn'. This means he is able to concentrate for longer training periods. He is also very familiar with the marker and reward, and watches you closely for instructions so he can get his treats faster!

Crawl

Crawling is a trick that takes a little time to perfect but looks really good. You can have your dog sneakily crawl under things or crawl up to people.

Step 1
Ask your dog to drop at your left side and gently place your left hand on top of his shoulders. Reassure him that he is a good dog at this point, to give him confidence about your hand being on his shoulders.

Step 2
With a piece of food in your right hand, gently lure your dog forward. If he goes to stand, apply a little pressure to his shoulders to keep him in the drop position.

Step 3
When your dog crawls one step forward, quickly mark and reward, letting him have the piece of food you have in your hand. Practise with just one or two steps forward at first and do this several times in one training session. Your aim here is to have the dog move forward in the crawl position and not stand up – not crawl for any distance at this stage. You are first getting the basic position and moves right.

Step 4

Again, set your dog up at your left side and lure him forward with a piece of food. You may still need to keep a little pressure on his shoulders. Now start to increase the length that he crawls, so that he is doing several steps in the crawling position.

Step 5

Once your dog is familiar with the exercise, you can introduce the word 'crawl'. Say 'crawl' as you begin to lure Fido forward with the food.

Step 6

At this point, you should be able to take your left hand from your dog's shoulders and he should crawl on command, lured by the food. If he stands up, go back to working with your hand on his shoulders for a few more training sessions to teach him to stay in the down position as he moves.

Step 7

Now remove the food from directly in front of the dog and simply use your hand to encourage him along by continuing to hold it close to his head. Mark and reward after he has crawled for several steps.

Step 8

Finally, work to move further away from your dog so that eventually, with practice, you will be able to ask him to crawl when you are some distance away from him.

Tip

Some dogs find it difficult to learn to get right down low when they crawl. To help them with this, try teaching them to crawl under an object like a table rather than placing a hand on their back. Just ensure that they do not have a physical condition that is making it hard for them to crawl, such as arthritis.

Wave

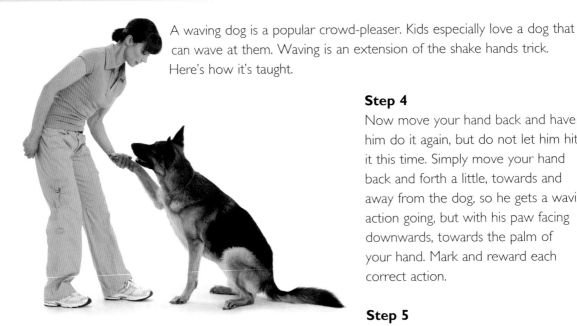

A waving dog is a popular crowd-pleaser. Kids especially love a dog that can wave at them. Waving is an extension of the shake hands trick. Here's how it's taught.

Step 1

Have your dog sit in front of you and begin by shaking hands, as you have taught earlier. Do a few hand shakes to get your dog targeting your hands with his paws and to get him concentrating on targeting.

Step 2

Choose one paw for your dog to wave and stick to it. Eventually, if you choose to, you can teach your dog to wave with both paws. However, start with one just as you did with the 'shake hands'.

Step 3

Do not use the 'shake hands' command. Just hold out the palm of your hand to the dog. If he targets your hand and hits it with his paw, mark and reward.

Step 4

Now move your hand back and have him do it again, but do not let him hit it this time. Simply move your hand back and forth a little, towards and away from the dog, so he gets a waving action going, but with his paw facing downwards, towards the palm of your hand. Mark and reward each correct action.

Step 5

Now work over several training sessions to turn your hand over, into a waving position. The idea is to have your dog targeting the palm of your hand with the pad of his paw. So as you turn your hand over, he will lift his paw.

Step 6

Once you have your dog waving well at you when you wave your hand directly in front of him, introduce the command 'wave'. Say 'wave' each time you do the trick for two or three training sessions, to establish a link with the word in your dog's mind.

Step 7

Next, you can work on gaining distance with this trick. Sit Fido in front of you again, but this time give him the 'stay' command.

Step 8

Now take a step backwards, say 'wave' and wave your hand. Your dog should wave from the short distance away. If he goes to move forward, say nothing but do not mark and reward. Set him up in front of you again and take a smaller step backwards.

Step 9

Work to gradually step further and further back from your dog so that eventually you can wave to him from some distance away and he will wave back. Sometimes the dog will lean forwards or try to stand up and wave at the same time. If this happens, just take a step or two backwards in your training and teach from where Fido is doing things correctly.

Step 10

If you wish, you can now begin to work on the other paw. Have the dog target your other hand with his other paw so that he learns to wave with both paws, depending on which hand you are waving with!

Tip

Rather than say the word 'wave', you may choose to say 'hi' or 'bye' instead. You will find that, with practice, you can say all three words and the dog will work off your hand signal anyway, waving to whichever word you say.

Which Hand?

With this trick, you can teach your dog two things at once. The first is you teach your dog to target your hand with a touch of his nose, on the command 'touch'. Once he can do this, you teach him to touch which hand has a treat in it. It's a doggy version of the 'penny under the cups' sideshow trick!

Step 1
Place a treat in your hand and clench the hand into a fist around the treat.

Step 2
Have your dog sit facing you and hold the hand with the treat out, in front of his nose. Have your hand about twenty centimetres (eight inches) away. Wait for Fido to smell the treat. If he does not reach forward with his nose, move your hand closer.

Step 3
When Fido reaches forward and touches your closed fist, immediately mark and open your hand so he can take the reward. Do this several times, until your dog reaches up and targets your closed fist with his nose each time.

Step 4
Each time you now do this trick say the word 'touch' when you offer your closed fist. You now have a dog that touches and targets your closed fist and you will find that you can guide him around with it, whether there is food in the fist or not. At this point you can ask for a touch and reward from the other hand or from your pocket, if you wish.

Step 5

Next, you begin the 'which hand?' part of this exercise. Once again, place a piece of food in your closed fist and have Fido sit facing you. Hold out your fist as usual but this time also hold out your other fist. Have the fist with the food in it much closer to your dog though, so he is encouraged to sniff and reach towards the correct one. Mark and reward each correct touch.

Step 6

Slowly move your second fist forward over a series of touches so that it is level with the hand with the food in it. Continue to mark and reward each correct touch. If Fido touches the wrong hand, just keep your hands still and say nothing, and wait until he touches the correct one. He will scent out the food and touch the correct one in a short time.

Step 7

Swap the food from fist to fist randomly, so that your dog learns the food might be in either fist.

Step 8

Once your dog is reliably touching either fist with his nose when you say 'touch' you can introduce a bit of sideshow patter. When Fido is sitting in front of you, turn away from him and swap the food from hand to hand. Ask him which hand he thinks the food is in before you say the word 'touch'. Then hold your fists out. Children also love this trick. Ask them if they can guess which hand the food is in too, and see who is correct more often – Fido or the children. Of course Fido will be, as he is the one with the excellent scenting capabilities that can detect even a tiny piece of food!

Tip

You can teach your dog to target your closed fists with his paws too, to identify which fist the food is in. Simply start at the beginning and squat down in front of him, asking for a paw touch before giving him the food.

Atishoo!

You can teach your best friend to get your handkerchief out of your pocket each time you sneeze and give it to you. This cool trick is actually a variation on the 'fetch and carry' exercise. You are teaching your dog to fetch an item from your pocket and then give it to you… just when you need to blow your nose. Therefore, you need to have taught your dog to fetch before you teach this exercise.

Step 1
Begin by choosing a large 'handkerchief'. A chequered cloth table napkin is ideal for this trick as it is about the size of a handkerchief but is thicker material, looks good and is easily visible to an audience when it is in your pocket.

Step 2
Sit your dog in front of you with the handkerchief in one of your hands and a treat in the other. Drop the handkerchief on the ground beside you and ask your dog to fetch it. Mark and reward when he does this.

Step 3
Repeat Step 2 several times so that your dog is reliably picking up the handkerchief and giving it to you. When he is at this stage, move on to Step 4.

Step 4
Pick up the handkerchief and hook the tip of it in the front pocket of your pants (you need to be wearing pants with pockets) so that the majority of it is hanging out. Make it really easy for your dog to get the handkerchief.

Step 5
Now ask Fido to 'fetch' again, turning your body so that it is almost impossible for him to miss grabbing the handkerchief. If he does not grab it immediately, encourage him by flapping the handkerchief about a little with your hand and repeating 'fetch'.

Step 6

When your dog is reliably taking the handkerchief from your pocket and giving it to you, push it further into your pocket so less is sticking out. You want just enough for an audience to see the handkerchief well and for it to come out of your pocket easily when Fido tugs on it. Mark and reward each time you do the trick, as usual.

Step 7

Once your dog has reached this stage, you can alter the word you use for the trick. Fido knows what to do, so do a couple using the word 'fetch'. Then you can change the word to 'atishoo' and turn your hip to him to encourage him to get the handkerchief again. If he does not take it and is confused, say the word 'fetch' followed by 'atishoo'. Then gradually say 'fetch' more and more quietly before ceasing to say the word altogether.

Step 8

Increase the way you say 'atishoo' and make it look more like you are genuinely sneezing. Then try walking as you are doing this and encourage your dog to grab the handkerchief as you are walking along. When he knows the trick really well you can also swap the handkerchief to your back pocket if you prefer.

Tip

For a variation on this trick, if you have a big dog you can train the dog to jump up on your chest after taking the handkerchief from your pocket. Giving you the handkerchief from that position looks a little like he is trying to wipe your nose for you!

Spin and Twist

Teaching your dog to spin in both directions looks very graceful. It is a good trick and is also used in doggy dancing, or 'canine freestyle'. This trick once again involves the dog targeting your hand – this time with his nose.

Step 1
Have your dog stand facing you with a piece of food in your right hand. Hold the food in front of his nose so that he is reaching for it.

Step 2
Slowly move your hand in a wide circle, in an anti-clockwise direction. Keep the food right in front of your dog's nose so that he follows the food. When he has slowly spun around in a full circle, mark and reward. Here you are luring him to spin around. Do this step several times, so that your dog becomes familiar with the act of anti-clockwise spinning.

Step 3
Now have no food in your hand. Simply hold your hand out and guide your dog around in the spin. Then once again mark and reward at the completion of the circle. Your dog should follow (target) your hand. If he does not, go back to Step 2 and do a few more spins with food in your hand as a lure.

Step 4
Once Fido is following your hand in an anti-clockwise direction quite confidently, you can name the trick. I call an anti-clockwise spin 'twist'. Repeat Step 3 but this time, say 'twist' as you begin to use your hand to get the dog to turn.

Step 5
As your dog becomes better at spinning in this direction, you can reduce your hand signal so that you make a small circular motion with your hand as you say 'twist' and Fido will automatically spin in an anti-clockwise direction. Continue to mark and reward after each spin.

Step 6

Once your dog is reliably spinning in one direction, begin to teach him to spin in the other. Begin from Step 1, teaching Fido to spin in a clockwise direction. The aim is to have your dog spin in both directions on a hand signal from your right hand.

Step 7

Be very clear with your hand movements with this exercise. Your dog needs to learn that when you turn your hand one way, he is to spin in one direction and when you turn it in the other, he is to spin the opposite way. Combined with the verbal signal, this works well as long as you are clear about it.

Step 8

When you have taught your dog to spin clockwise, introduce the word 'spin'. Ensure you say both words 'spin' and 'twist' very clearly.

Step 9

Once your dog can spin and twist in both directions well on a small circular hand signal, try asking him for a combined spin and twist before you mark and reward. Ask him to spin one way and then immediately the other. This looks great. You can also ask him to do more than one spin or twist in a row before marking and rewarding. This is called 'chaining' behaviours in dog training – meaning more than one behaviour is performed to complete an exercise.

Tip

The spin and twist can also be performed with your dog at your side, or as you are walking along. When trying this, go back to making your hand signals much larger so that Fido does not get confused by the change of position or extra movement.

Toys in the Toy Box

With this trick you can have a tidy dog that puts his own toys away. It is not a hard trick but does take a while to perfect. You will need a wooden or cardboard box about the size of a milk crate (or a milk crate itself) and a few of Fido's favourite toys.

Step 1
Place the box in an area of low distraction like your living room floor and put one toy beside the box. Make sure it is a toy that your dog is familiar with and happy to pick up.

Step 2
Now put your hand down to the toy and encourage Fido to pick it up. Use the 'hold and carry' exercise you taught him earlier, to assist.

Step 3
When your dog is holding the toy, guide him with your hand to place it into the box. As soon as he puts it into the box, mark and reward. Do this over the box, so that the dog's attention is focused on the area inside the box as you give the treat. This helps your dog to quickly learn that the toy needs to be put accurately in the box in order to gain a reward. Repeat this step for a number of training sessions until your dog is reliably picking up the toy and putting it into the box without a lot of encouragement from you to do so.

Step 4
Now you can introduce a command to the exercise. You could say 'toy box', for example, when you want the dog to put his toys in the box.

Step 5
At this point, take a step away from your dog and the toy box, and work to gradually step further and further back until he is putting a single toy in the toy box on a command. Then mark the correct action as you step forward and reward him over the box.

Step 6

Introduce a second familiar toy to the trick. Place two toys on the floor and return to standing quite close to the box. When your dog has put one toy in the box on command, mark and reward. Then encourage him to put the second toy in too. Mark and reward again.

Step 7

When your dog is putting two toys into the box reliably, cut out the first mark and reward and wait until he has put the two toys in before you reward. Do this before you step away from the box again.

Step 8

Again, once the dog is working well with two toys build distance between yourself and the box.

Step 9

Follow the previous steps each time you add a toy. As you and your dog progress you will find he picks up adding the extra toy much quicker and it will take you less time to add extra toys to the exercise. Over time he will be able to pick up a number of toys and put them all in the box before being rewarded.

Tip

This technique can be used to teach your dog to put other items in other things. For example, the dog can be taught to put a soft toy into a doll bed, or papers into a wastepaper basket.

Jump through a Hoop

Many dogs just love to jump! You can teach your dog to jump through a hoop, or even use this technique to teach him to jump through a bicycle tyre, or over hurdles. You will need to get a plastic hula hoop for this trick.

Step 3
Call your dog from the stay and encourage him to walk through the hoop. The moment he does, mark and reward. Repeat Steps 1 to 3 a few times until Fido completely understands what he must do.

Step 4
Now that your dog understands what to do, you can introduce a command. You can choose any word, but 'through' or 'hoop' are good ones. Give your chosen command after you call your dog from the stay. So you might say, 'Fido, come' and then 'hoop'.

Step 1
Ask your dog to sit and stay, then walk a short distance from him with the hula hoop in your hand. One metre (three feet) is quite sufficient at this stage.

Step 2
Face your dog and place the edge of the hula hoop on the ground so that he does not actually have to jump, but simply has to walk through it.

Step 5
Now take a step back so that you and the hoop are further away from your dog, but still keep the hoop on the ground. Mark and reward each time he goes through it and work slowly backwards until you have a distance of a few metres (yards) between you and your dog.

Step 6
Raise the hula hoop a few centimetres (one to two inches) off the ground and call your dog through it. Mark and reward when he has gone through it, as usual. Don't be tempted to increase the height of the hoop too quickly, or he may feel unsure and have a setback. This especially applies to smaller dogs.

Step 7

At each training session, raise the hoop a little further and further off the ground. For medium-sized dogs that are very agile, such as Border Collies, you can, with practice, end up with the hoop at shoulder height.

Step 8

When your dog is practised at jumping through the hoop, you can quickly swing around after the first jump and ask him to jump back the other way too. This looks quite spectacular!

Tips

Check with your vet before teaching your dog to jump any significant heights. It is also very important to consider your dog's age before teaching him to jump. If you have a pup, larger breeds should not do a lot of jumping until they are at least twelve months of age because of their growing joints. Older dogs may injure themselves by jumping a lot.

PART THREE
TOP TRICKS

By the time you reach this section you and your dog will have no doubt built up quite a show of amusing tricks for friends and family. As well as this, you will probably have found that your dog is generally more obedient and has a stronger bond with you than previously, due to the fact that he enjoys the time you spend working together.

Now you can tackle some of these harder tricks together. See how far you can get – there's always more to learn!

Slam Dunk

Yes, your dog can play basketball too! You can teach him that when you pass him a ball, he needs to run and put it through a mini basketball hoop. This is great fun for you and your dog, and any spectators. You will need a child's basketball hoop, or a small 'office basketball' hoop, and a ball the size of a tennis ball or slightly larger.

Step 1
Stand with your dog right beside the basketball hoop and have it low, at the dog's head height. Have him hold the ball in his mouth.

Step 2
Use your hand to guide the dog to the hoop and encourage him to drop the ball through it. The moment he does, mark and reward. Repeat this step several times, until your dog can easily drop the ball through the hoop from right beside it.

Step 3
Now add the words 'slam dunk' or 'through the hoop' or another suitable phrase to the exercise, as you give the ball to Fido.

Step 4
At this point, leave your dog close to the hoop but take a step back yourself and throw the ball to your dog before asking him to slam dunk it. The hoop should still be at the height of the dog's head. Mark and then step forward and reward when he drops the ball through the hoop.

Step 5

Now position your dog a short distance away from the hoop and then move a metre (three feet) or so away from both dog and hoop yourself before throwing the ball to him. Work over several training sessions to increase the distance you and your dog are from the hoop and also change positions around the hoop.

Step 6

When Fido is very comfortable with putting the ball in the hoop when it is thrown to him and when he is given the command, you can begin to slightly increase the height of the hoop. You can make the hoop a height that suits the size and agility of your dog but, as a general rule, don't make it too high or too difficult for your dog to reach up and drop the ball in or he will not enjoy doing the trick.

Step 7

Now is the time to make a real game of it! Begin to run around a little and encourage Fido to chase you. Throw the ball to him from a run and then ask him to slam dunk it. You put the ball through the hoop too. Play 'one on one' with him. You will find that this game is so enjoyable for the dog that you don't need to mark and reward each correct placement of the ball through the hoop. Playing the game itself is a big enough reward.

Step 8

You can also have your dog slam dunk the ball and then pick it up and bring it back to you. Teach him by using the 'fetch' command after he has slam dunked the ball.

Tip
You can also teach your dog to place quoits on a ring and 'play quoits' with you, using the same training method.

Get the Phone

This fun retrieval trick has applications in the 'real world'. Assistance dogs are able to bring the phone for their owners and this is a variation on the exercise. You will need to get a child's toy mobile phone or an old cordless phone if you do the trick inside. To do this trick, Fido needs to have learnt the retrieval and 'speak' exercises in Part One.

Step 1
Have your dog sit and offer the phone handset to him as you say 'fetch'. Mark and reward if he takes the phone in his mouth. By this stage, most dogs will take the phone but, if not, run through the 'hold and carry' exercise on page 22 to make him comfortable with holding it. Make the phone ring while you are doing this too, to accustom him to the sound.

Step 2
Put the phone down on the floor in front of the dog and make it ring. As you do so, tell him to 'fetch'. Mark and reward if Fido picks the phone up and brings it to you.

Step 3
When your dog is reliably bringing the ringing phone to you from directly in front of you, you can decide to either change the 'fetch' to 'get the phone' or some such phrase, or you can say nothing and work to make the cue for Fido to get the phone the sound of the ringing itself. If you wish to have your dog pick the phone up purely on the sound of the ring, fade the word 'fetch' by saying it quietly and then not saying it at all. Give your dog a chance to move towards the phone if it rings, and then mark and reward if he does so on his own. He will generally go and pick it up without the word 'fetch' the next time.

Step 4

At this point, you can slowly move the phone handset further away from your dog at each training session.

Step 5

Now you can really have some fun with this trick. Try teaching your dog to speak into the phone himself! When Fido brings the phone to you, have him sit in front of you and mark and reward, as usual.

Step 6

Pretend to answer the phone and say to your dog, 'It's for you!' Then hold the phone out to your dog and tell him to speak. Mark and reward as soon as he barks into the phone.

Step 7

Repeat the above steps several times and you will soon find your dog 'speaks' into the phone as soon as you hold it out to him. You have now chained several behaviours together – running to the phone, retrieving it, sitting in front of you and speaking into the phone on cue!

Step 8

If your dog speaks before you hold out the phone to him, simply do not mark the behaviour and reward. Wait until he is quiet again and then ask him to speak. Reward correct behaviours only.

Tips

You may wish to teach your dog this trick so he brings the real phone to you when it rings. If so, just ensure that he does not accidentally crunch it. Teach him at the 'hold' stage to be gentle by marking and rewarding quiet holding and no chewing.

Counting

Your dog also needs to speak for this clever trick, where it looks as though he can actually add up! It is a great crowd-pleaser and when you get expert with your hand signals, even adults sometimes have trouble working out how it's done.

Step 1

For this trick, we will introduce a hand signal to ask your dog to speak, instead of using the word. Sit your dog in front of you and say 'speak'. As you do, very clearly hold out your right hand with the index finger pointing towards the dog. The dog must be able to see the visual cue (the hand signal) at the same time as the verbal cue (the word 'speak'). Mark and reward for speaking – as long as the dog only barks once. This is very important. If the dog gives more than one bark, do not mark and reward. Say nothing and try again.

Step 2

Practise Step 1 over several training sessions. Make sure your dog can clearly see your hand signal with one finger sticking out in front of him. Then, try asking him to speak with the hand signal only. You will find that he will speak just on the hand signal now. If he does not, simply practise Step 1 for a little longer.

Step 3

Now you have your dog barking once on a hand signal where you are pointing your index finger at him, it is time to try for two barks. Here you need to go back a step and introduce the word 'speak' again. This time, show Fido your hand with your index finger and middle finger clearly pointing at him. Chances are, Fido will bark once. At this point do not mark and reward but say 'speak'. When Fido barks again, mark and reward.

Step 4

At this point, your dog will bark once on a single-fingered hand signal and twice on a two-fingered signal, if you include the word 'speak' after the first bark. Practise over several training sessions to have him bark twice for two fingers, and gradually stop saying 'speak' to achieve the second bark.

Step 5

It is very important that you encourage your dog to understand that he hasn't simply swapped barking once for barking twice, but needs to observe your hand signals. In order to keep him barking once on a single-fingered signal, practise barking once at individual sessions and then practise both barking once and barking twice at the same session when your dog is competently barking twice.

Tip

Dogs respond very readily to both visual and verbal cues and you can use them in combination or on their own for lots of tricks.

Step 6

When your dog has perfected barking twice on a two-fingered signal you can move on to three, four and five, repeating the steps from the beginning as shown. Some dogs become confused after five barks but some will bark more times if you use both hands for signals. It all depends on how much you practise!

Step 7

Once you have perfected the number of barks on a hand signal you want your dog to do, you can work on reducing the signal. Make it smaller and quicker. The idea is that your dog sees the hand signal but an audience will not so readily pick it. Then you can say something like 'What's one and one, Fido?' and make the signal, and Fido will bark twice. It makes him look very clever!

Run to a Mark and Pose

This trick is a good one if you want to take photos of your dog, or if you are thinking of doing TV work with him. It involves the use of the basic shake hands targeting trick. You will need a square of carpet around forty by forty centimetres (sixteen by sixteen inches).

Step 4
At this point, introduce the words 'on your mark'. Say to the dog 'on your mark' and then hold the carpet square out for him to hit.

Step 5
When Fido is hitting the carpet square each time you hold it out and give him the command, place it on the ground right at your feet. Say 'on your mark' again and he should still touch it with his paw. If he does not, take a step backwards and reinforce that he must touch the carpet with his paw on the command.

Step 1
Sit your dog in front of you with the carpet square in one hand.

Step 2
Hold the carpet square in front of you and say nothing, but hold your other hand out for your dog to shake. When your dog lifts his paw, move the carpet square so that he hits it. Mark and reward immediately.

Step 3
Repeat this several times until the dog understands that he must target the carpet square and touch it with his paw. If he shakes hands competently this will happen quickly. Mark and reward after each correct action.

Step 6

Now that Fido is reliably touching the carpet square with his paw when it is on the ground, ask him to stay when he is on it. You can also try 'wait' or 'freeze'. You are training him to hold very still in that position. When he reliably holds a standing position with his paw on the carpet for several seconds, you can move on to the next step.

Step 7

Slowly move the carpet square further away from you over several training sessions. When you do this, don't work on Fido holding his position. Work on increasing distance in one training session. Then work on holding position for longer in the next session, without trying to further increase distance. Do not try to work on two criteria at once or Fido will get confused.

Step 8

Eventually, work towards having the carpet square around ten metres (eleven yards) away from you, and your dog holding position for as long as you ask him to, until you mark and reward.

Step 9

Finally, when you have everything else working well, gradually cut down the carpet square bit by bit over a large number of training sessions until it is the size of a jam jar lid. Do not rush this – you may want to keep it at one size for a week or so before you cut another piece off. With practice, your dog will easily target something very small and hold position.

Tips

Dogs used in film and TV work are sometimes trained to stand on targets the size of a twenty-cent piece. This way their paw covers the target and it cannot be seen by the cameras.

Go Shopping

Teach your dog to carry a basket to an item, put the item in the basket and then carry the basket back to you. This trick requires a number of steps for your dog to perfect, but it is a real show-stopper. You need to teach carrying the basket and putting an item in the basket as two separate exercises. You will need a wicker basket with a handle and an item such as a dog toy or chewy bone.

Step 1

First you must teach your dog to put the item into the basket. Place the basket on the floor in front of your dog. Then put the item on the floor beside the basket and ask the dog to fetch and hold it.

Step 2

Use your hand to guide the dog to place the item in the basket. As soon as he does this, mark and reward over the basket to keep his attention focused on where he needs to put the toy (as you did for the simpler 'toys in the toy box' trick on page 36).

Step 3

When your dog is reliably placing the item into the basket, move back from it and let him do it himself, without any guiding. Then mark correct actions, step forward and reward. Do this until you are several metres (yards) away from the dog.

Step 4

Now train your dog to carry the basket. He may do this readily, or you may need to refer back to the 'hold and carry' exercises on page 22 to make him comfortable with carrying it. Do this as a separate exercise at separate training sessions. Before you proceed further, make sure your dog can confidently pick the basket up, carry it a short distance and put it down.

Step 5

At this stage you can begin to do these exercises together. Place the basket very close to the item on the floor. Have your dog pick up the basket and carry it over to the toy. Initially, walk with your dog. Mark and reward for this first step.

Step 9

Finally, chain the three steps by removing the mark and reward from, first, the act of carrying the basket out to the item and then bringing it back to you. Then remove the words in between each step. Replace the first word by saying something like 'go shopping' followed by 'carry' and then remove the 'carry' slowly over time.

Step 10

This trick takes some time to perfect. It also pays to go back to basics every now and then and train each part of the trick separately, to keep it sharp and to keep your dog motivated to do all parts of the trick happily.

Step 6

Have your dog put the item in the basket and mark and reward again.

Step 7

Now have your dog pick up the basket and you run backwards, encouraging him to run to you with the basket in his mouth. Mark and reward again.

Step 8

Work to slowly move the basket back over several training sessions. Then stand further back and let the dog perform the actions without you at his side. Still mark and reward each separate stage of the trick.

> *Tip*
>
> *When your dog is good at this trick you can train him to put two items in the basket. This requires you to go back to Steps 2 and 3.*

Marching

Having your dog march beside you is a trick that looks spectacular and everyone loves to see it. Teaching your dog to march is a development of the simple 'shake hands' trick on page 14. Here's how to do it:

Step 1
Stand your dog in front of you and reach down and ask him to shake hands.

Do this with both paws – your left hand shaking his right paw and your right hand shaking his left paw, as shown in the 'shake hands' trick. Mark and reward as usual.

Step 2
Now open up your hands when you ask for a shake, so that the dog targets the flat of each hand, rather than you actually shaking his paws. Practise this for at least one training session.

Step 3
Next, gently lift your left foot when you lift your left hand, so it is directly below your hand as your dog paws at your hand. Do the same with your right hand and foot. Mark and reward each correct behaviour.

Step 4
Slowly, over a few training sessions, remove your hands so that the dog is now targeting your foot, and touching each foot with his paw rather than the hand.

Step 5
At this point, you need to move away from the dog a little. Lift your feet and when the dog lifts his paws, pull your feet back slightly so he misses touching them. Mark and reward when your dog lifts his paws at the same time as you lift your feet, but does not touch your feet. Show him what you want through careful marking and rewarding.

Step 6
When your dog is competently lifting his feet in time to yours on the spot as you stand in front of him, add the words 'left' and 'right' to the trick. Ensure that you teach him HIS left and right, not yours as you are facing him. Do this over several training sessions so he clearly understands the verbal cues of left and right. Mark and reward each lift of a paw.

Step 7

Change your position so your dog is now on your left. This is one of the hardest parts of the exercise for your dog because you are now going to swap your feet, as well as stand in a different place. You will be lifting the same leg as he does from now on. Be sure he fully understands the commands 'left' and 'right' before you do this.

Step 8

Give your dog the 'left' command and raise your left leg. If he raises the wrong leg, go back to helping him a little with your hands to give him the idea. Mark and reward any correct or even tentative lift of the paw. Work through this stage little by little, on the spot.

Step 9

Once your dog is marching well on the spot, you can begin to move forward. To keep your dog in place at your side, you may need to lure him at first with a piece of food in your left hand. Mark and reward each correct paw lift and correct marching position.

Step 10

You can now begin to mark and reward every second or third lift of the paw over several training sessions. Soon your dog will be able to march for quite a number of steps before you mark and reward, making a good marching line.

Tip

Marching is a trick often used in dog dancing, in combination with many other moves.

Take My Socks Off

Cheeky dogs just love this trick as they get to play with their owner's socks! Again the dog will use the skills he has previously learnt to fetch and carry objects – even though he is not carrying your socks far. Use a pair of thick socks for this trick so that Fido does not accidentally nip your toes when he is learning it. You will need a chair to sit on too.

Step 1
First, take one sock and play a little tug with your dog. Previously you may have told your dog not to touch your clothing and shoes. Now you need to let him know it is okay with THIS pair of socks. Play until your dog is confidently tugging at the sock.

Step 2
At the next training session, place the sock on the ground near the chair. Then sit on the chair with your dog at your side and ask him to fetch the sock. When he does, mark and reward the exercise. Repeat this several times, each time bringing the sock a little closer to the chair.

Step 3
End each session with a very short game of tug with the sock, to keep your dog interested in tugging at the sock. If he does not want to give the sock back to you, swap it for a treat. You need to keep up Fido's interest in tugging the sock because he will eventually have to tug the sock off your foot.

Step 4
Work over several training sessions to get the sock closer and closer to you until it is partly on your foot. Now that the sock is partly on your foot your dog will have to tug slightly to get it off. The first time he does this, mark and reward and then praise him extravagantly, as the further the sock goes on your foot the harder it will be for him to pull it off.

Step 5

Continue to place the sock further and further onto your foot, until your dog is pulling off a sock that is fully on. Once you have reached this stage, you can change the name of the exercise from Fetch to something like 'take my socks off, Fido'. Do this by saying the phrase first and then adding 'fetch'. Then gradually remove the word 'fetch' over several training sessions.

Step 6

Once you have your dog reliably taking off one sock on command, introduce a second sock on your other foot. You will not need to place it far away, as this exercise has already been taught. All you are asking is for Fido to do it twice.

Step 7

Have your dog take one sock off, then mark and reward. Point to the other sock and repeat the phrase 'take my socks off, Fido'. Mark and reward again, after the second sock has been removed. You now have two separate behaviours being marked and rewarded.

Step 8

Once Fido is reliably and quickly taking both socks off, finish this trick by chaining the two sock removals together without the reward and second command in the middle. Simply do not reward for the first sock removal but encourage your dog to move straight to the second sock.

Step 9

Once this is achieved, remove the second command. Then Fido will remove both socks on the one command of 'take my socks off, Fido'.

Tip

You could add to this trick by then having your dog retrieve your slippers.

Simple Sniffing Fun

Dogs are well known for their incredible sense of smell. Everyone knows how our canine friends can be trained in search and rescue and as police tracker dogs, but did you know you can use Fido's sense of smell to do some fun tricks? Try this simple one to start with.

Find It, Fido

For this trick, you will drop a small article such as a pen or a piece of tube on the ground and have your dog find it, using his nose to retrace your footsteps.

Step 1

First, choose an article and teach your dog to fetch by throwing it and having him retrieve it, as shown earlier in this book.

Step 2

Now find a grassy open area that you have not walked on and begin by having your dog walk along at your side for about ten paces. Drop the article as you walk and make sure he sees you do it. In addition, make sure you have held the article in your hands for a little while before you drop it, so your personal smell will be on it.

Step 3

Turn around and tell your dog to 'fetch it'. Point to the article as you do this. At this stage it is not so much about Fido sniffing out the article but about building his confidence that he is able to locate and find the article. At the moment, he will be purely using his sight to find it. Mark and reward and give lots of praise when he returns to you with the article.

Step 4

Practise Step 3 over several training sessions, each time extending the distance you walk by a pace or two. When doing more than one 'seek back' per session, make sure you walk over new ground – that you are not crossing the place where you walked before as this will confuse your dog.

Step 5

When your dog is confidently walking around fifteen metres (sixteen yards) before you send him to fetch the article, try turning a corner. Shorten the distance you walk again and let him see the article once again so that the corner does not confuse him. At this stage you will see him put his head to the ground and start to use his nose, as well as his eyes, to find the article. Continue to mark and reward each return.

Step 6

At this point, start trying to drop the article without your dog seeing exactly when you do it. Make sure you do not walk too far at this stage. Give him every chance to 'win' so that he continues to be confident in the trick.

Step 7

Keep building on this at every training session until you can drop an article and walk many metres (yards) with a few turns before you send your dog to find it.

Step 8

Now try having someone else drop the article for you, as you and Fido walk away. Have the person hold the article with kitchen tongs, so they do not contaminate the article with their smell. You only want your smell on it as that is what your dog is searching for.

Step 9

Try teaching your dog to hold objects like a bunch of keys or a wallet and then do this trick. It will come in very handy should you ever drop your keys when out in a park somewhere!

Tip

Ten per cent of a dog's brain is dedicated to smell. In humans, this is only one per cent! Dogs are able to detect smells at levels around a hundred million times lower than we are able to.

Pick a Colour

Take your time when teaching this advanced scenting trick, which relies on your dog picking out a red plastic block that has your scent on it. Children in particular love this trick and they have to think hard to work out how it's done. You will need ten children's plastic blocks of different colours, one of which is red. Have a few spare red ones too, in case your dog chews the one he regularly picks up.

Step 3

Ask your dog to fetch the red block. Initially, you may need to stand with him and use your hand to guide him to pick up the block you want. Mark and reward the instant he does this. If he brings you the wrong block still offer lots of encouragement to keep him feeling confident, just don't mark and reward.

Step 1

To begin, teach your dog to retrieve a single plastic block, using the 'fetch' method shown earlier in the book. Make it a fun, playful exercise.

Step 2

Put a red block on the ground a metre (yard) or two from your sitting dog. Make sure you have held it in your hands for a while. You can make it even easier for your dog initially by putting the scent of a treat on it too, but make sure your smell is on the block from your hands. Place another block beside it using kitchen tongs, so it has none of your personal scent on it.

Step 4

Now take a step back and ask your dog to fetch the red block on his own. Still just have two blocks there. Remember not to touch any of the blocks yourself, except the red one. Use tongs to move the other block around so your smell does not contaminate it.

Step 5

When your dog smells the blocks and brings you the red block every time, add a third block. Repeat Steps 3 and 4, being careful to mark and reward correctly and give your dog huge praise for bringing the correct block to you.

Step 8

If you wish, you can stop adding the smell of a treat to the red block at this stage and just use your personal scent.

Step 9

Now add a bit of sideshow patter to this trick for an audience. Talk to Fido and ask him what his favourite colour is. Pretend he says red. Then ask him to go and choose the red block from the line. Send him and of course he will, as the red one has your scent on it. It has nothing to do with him seeing the colours and relies totally on his scenting capabilities. People love to watch this and figure out how it's done.

Step 6

Take your time adding blocks in a line with about ten centimetres (four inches) space in between them. Each time your dog becomes proficient at choosing the correct block from a group of two, three, four etc. and you add a block, go back to standing close to the blocks in case he needs any assistance. The idea is for Fido not to fail and get confused or lose confidence at any stage in what he is being asked to do.

Step 7

When you have added all blocks, you should have a line of ten coloured blocks with only one red one. Wash the blocks in warm water every so often to remove any extra smells and wash your old scent off the red block. Air the blocks and then store them in a plastic box when they are dry so they cannot be contaminated by other smells.

> ### Tip
>
> This trick takes some weeks to perfect but it is worth it. You can have fun with other articles too. Get some plastic letters and scent different ones. Teach your dog to spell 'dog' etc. Get some plastic animals and teach Fido to find the dog!

Target Sticks and Tricks

You can train your dog to target, or follow, your hand with his nose as shown on page 30 for the 'which hand?' trick. This is a very useful trick to teach because you can then use your hand to guide your dog to do things such as walk at your side, spin in circles and walk backwards. However, at some point you will want to take your hand away and have your dog perform these tricks without focusing on it. This can be difficult, as you can't remove your hand altogether.

Because of this, many dog trainers use a tool called a target stick to teach tricks. A target stick can be slowly removed, or faded, as the dog becomes proficient at the trick or exercise you are teaching – unlike your hand. So the stick is an extension of your hand that Fido focuses on, but it will eventually disappear, leaving only the trick you have taught – generally on a verbal command from you.

A target stick can be many things (you can teach your dog to target almost anything). Generally, a rod between forty and seventy centimetres (sixteen and twenty-eight inches) long with a round piece on its end is ideal. People also use items as diverse as a child's magic wand, a wooden spoon or even an old car aerial (which can be folded smaller and smaller as the dog becomes proficient at the trick you are teaching).

Try making a target stick out of one of these objects. A piece of dowel or curtain rod also works well. Tape a round object to the end of it, slightly larger than a fifty-cent piece. Choose your target stick and use it consistently throughout your dog's training sessions.

You can teach your dog some of the tricks featured earlier with a target stick, or go on and teach him new ones with it. Here's how to teach Fido about the stick.

Step 1

Have your dog stand in front of you and then hold the end of the target stick close up to his nose. Say nothing – just wait quietly.

Step 2

Being naturally curious, your dog will most likely reach forward and sniff the end of the stick. If he does not, wave the stick around a little to attract his attention. The second he touches the end of it, mark and reward. Timing is everything here! Make sure you get it right so Fido knows just what he has been rewarded for. Repeat this several times.

Step 3

When your dog is reliably touching the end of the target stick and being marked and rewarded every time for it, move the stick back from him a little way. Again, say nothing. No command will be introduced with the target stick as in this case it is just a tool to teach your dog to do other tricks.

Step 4

By this stage your dog knows he will get a reward if he touches the end of the target stick so he will step forward and reach for it. The moment he touches it, mark and reward again. If he seems confused and does not do so then move the end of the stick slightly closer to him.

Step 5

When your dog is completely familiar with the target stick, you can move it around and he will follow it in order to reach it and touch it, and get a reward. It is a very effective way of teaching him to move into different positions.

Step 6

You can also teach your dog to hold his nose still against the end of the stick by marking and rewarding for longer holds.

Target Sticks and Tricks (cont'd)

Here is a selection of tricks that you could train using a target stick, once you have taught your dog how to target one.

Bow

Follow the instructions on page 18. However, instead of using a treat as a lure to have your dog go into a bow position, you can lower the target stick between his two front paws and towards his chest so he reaches for it with his nose. This will put him in the bow position on the stick. Once he has achieved the correct position, mark and reward as usual. You can have him hold the bow position for a few seconds by keeping the target stick still so he presses his nose against it. When your dog is bowing well, introduce the command 'bow'. When you have done this for several training sessions slowly fade the target stick by shortening it in your hand and then pulling it away intermittently and just using the verbal cue 'bow'. You will find that Fido soon bows well without the stick and just on the word.

Spin and Twist

Here is another trick that is easily taught with a target stick. Follow the instructions on page 34 but instead of luring your dog with a piece of food, hold the target stick in front of him at his head height. Slowly move it around in an anti-clockwise direction.

Mark and reward when he has completed one full circle. When your dog is competently following the target stick around, introduce the command 'spin' for several training sessions. Then fade the target stick by shortening it in your hand and pulling it away intermittently and finally removing it altogether. Fido will then spin on the command alone. Repeat this procedure for the clockwise circle, or the twist.

Marching

Marching is a great trick to teach with a target stick because in the traditional way of teaching it, you must encourage the dog to swap position to the side when targeting your feet from a position in front of you. This sometimes leads to the dog reaching over with his left paw to still try to touch your feet, giving him a crooked march for a time until he becomes more experienced. With a target stick, you do not have this problem.

Step 1

First, teach the dog to target a specific stick with his paws, rather than his nose. Use a stick that looks significantly different from the stick you use for 'nose targeting' so that the dog can tell this is the one for 'paw targeting'.

Step 2

Sit your dog in front of you and tickle one of his paws with the end of the stick. Wait until Fido paws at the stick, then mark and reward. Do this for both paws over several training sessions, until your dog is targeting the stick with his paws the way he does for the 'shake hands' trick on page 14.

Step 3

Now stand your dog at your side and hold the target stick in front of his left paw. As he targets it, raise your left foot. Repeat for several training sessions. Then work on the right foot.

Step 4

Now add the words 'left' and 'right' as described in the original marching trick.

Step 5

Finally, fade the target stick as described on the previous page and your dog will be marching!

> ### Tip
>
> Target sticks are used around the world by other animal trainers too. They are used to move animals from place to place in zoos and to train marine mammals such as dolphins.

Problem Solving

When training your dog you will sometimes strike problems. Don't become disheartened, as this happens to the best trainers and their dogs. Here are some problems you may encounter and possible ways to solve them.

Question: *My dog is very good at bowing but he often bows at me when I am asking him to try something new. How do I stop this?*

Answer: When a dog doesn't quite understand what you are asking, he will often offer a well-understood behaviour to try to get his reward. To stop this, simply do not give any reaction to your dog bowing unless you actually ask for a bow. Then take a step back with the new behaviour you are teaching, or try a slightly different approach that is less confusing for the dog.

Question: *I am trying to teach my dog to crawl. We do lots of long training sessions but he does not seem to want to do the trick and gets up and tries to walk away. What can I do?*

Answer: First, check with your vet that your dog is fit and it is not hurting him to try to crawl. If he is okay, it may be that your training sessions are too long and he is becoming bored. Try shorter and more frequent training sessions.

Question: *My dog performs tricks very well in our back garden when we are alone but if I ask him to do them in front of others or do them at the park he makes mistakes. How do I solve this problem?*

Answer: When teaching your dog something new, always start in a place of low distraction like the backyard. When you go to the park or there are others around, the distractions make it harder for Fido to concentrate on what he is doing. Make sure he performs the tricks well in the backyard first and then take him to the park or somewhere with other people around and work from the beginning again. Start at a distance from other people and gradually move in closer. As Fido becomes used to working in a new place, he will be able to do the tricks again.

Question: My dog has just learnt to do the 'run to a mark and pose' trick. He was doing it well from a distance last week but suddenly he does not seem to be able to remember it any more. What can I do?

Answer: There could be many reasons for this problem but the most likely one is that he had not learnt the basics of this trick well enough before he moved on to the next step. He could also have accidentally had something wrong, like running too far or moving on the spot, marked and rewarded. To fix this problem go right back to the beginning of the trick and teach it from scratch. It will not take long at all to do this as your dog already knows the trick but it will eliminate or 'overwrite' whatever is causing the problem. Even when tricks are going well it pays to go back and start from the beginning every now and again, just to refresh the dog's memory and eliminate any little errors that are creeping into the trick.

Question: It seems to take my dog a long time to learn anything I try to teach him. He gets easily confused and makes a lot of mistakes before he gets any part of a trick right. Why is this happening?

Answer: Look at the timing of your marker word or sound and reward. How accurate are you with it? If you do not mark the exact action you want when Fido does it and you wait longer than a second, he will not understand what he has just been rewarded for. Work on refining this with simple exercises like sit and shake hands to build the dog's confidence too.

Question: I want to tell my dog he is doing something correctly without marking and rewarding, and therefore ending the exercise. How do I do this?

Answer: Simply use another word for approval that does not have a reward following it. The most common word to use is generally 'good'. This is because we have often already taught our dogs this. The phrase 'good dog' is one we say a lot. Fido will keep going, waiting for the marker word or sound and his reward but he will know he is doing the right thing.

About the Author

Heather Hammonds is the author of more than 120 books, both fiction and non-fiction. She also works as a dog trainer, helping people with their problem dogs, and was a voluntary dog obedience instructor for some years. Heather was a veterinary nurse for 15 years, working with vets to help all sorts of pets. She is passionate about animals and has spent her life working with and training them – everything from sulphur-crested cockatoos to mules and donkeys.

Heather is the proud owner of two purebred German Shepherd dogs – Tess, who features in this book, and Dunja, the 'baby sister' of the family who hopes to follow in Tess' pawsteps. Heather trains her two dogs to compete in obedience trials and tracking trials (where the dog must track down a person for up to 1.2 kilometres). She also trains both in tricks and dog dance. Heather believes that it is a privilege to work with her dogs and that each day brings new learning about how they think and how to train them and, most important of all, how to have fun with them.

Tess (kennel name Melkirra Jade) is a four-year-old German Shepherd dog. Tess likes nothing better than to be out and about working with her handler, and she spends around twenty hours a week doing this. She is the proud holder of two Australian National Kennel Council titles – Companion Dog (obedience award) and Tracking Dog (tracking award) – and is currently working towards further titles.

Her favourite pastimes when not working are going for long bushwalks, swims at the beach, playing ball with her handler, playing with her 'little sister' in the backyard…and snoozing on the couch!